AMERICAN BESTIARY

DIEGO MAENZA

Translated by Gastón Jofre Torres

www.traduzionelibri.it
www.diegomaenza.com

AMERICAN BESTIARY

DIEGO MAENZA

Translated by Gastón Jofre Torres

SOUTH AMERICA

THE COVERED LADY

(Romantic quintet of a beheaded Ecuadorian)

Nupcial poison in
the death rattle of drunkenness.
You howl the pain that escapes from your pores
when you unmask your teeth
and you feel the caress of Tánatos.

Rain of spilled dark prisms.
Rotten vulva that numbs the fellatio.
Who kissed you attest your fragrance,
but the ones you touched are dead;
ergo, I have spoken with death.

Narrow alleys revere you,
mother of darkness, wife of sleep,
sulfur lover, friend of the anthracite.
The magnolia expels sweat from your uterus:
breaks Ecuadorian avenues like carrion.

You distract the young man and the old man in the
same way.
Your philosophical postulates: sex and revenge.
Who saw you legitimize your beauty,
but now they are clergymen or they are in the
asylums;
ergo, I've talked to the harlots.

One night, drunk with love, I caught up with you.
I found you black as silicon
and I was pale as a pond

that will reflect the moon of your sex.
Suicide is the purest form of love.

THE MUQUI

(Human poem of a Peruvian miner)

I belong to the mines.
At dawn everything ends and everything begins.
The corollary of cripples is a song of pain.
I chew a coca leaf while I masturbate
ruminating on the paralysis of materialism.

I am elusive even though my cousins are gregarious
and circulate through the streams like a swarm of
hilarity.
I have decoded their Quipus and passions,
I have studied gold and man.

I belong to the water
that even washes the darkest corners:
a miner goes by with his stinky armpits,
it crashes its head against a very black stone.
How to talk after the categorical closure
if her children, young men and nymphs have not
eaten?

I do not have a neck: how to explain existentialism?
They shiver: shout coldness; they scream: they eat
hunger.
I wear my poncho: how to believe in the God of the
Sun if he leaves us?
Like mosses: how to trust Huiracocha if there is no corn?
I wear a hat: how to move forward if they exchange
our ideas?
I am little: human nature sucks

as much as the nature of the gods.
I stink, you stink, and so on to infinity.

I am the Murik that gives the freedom
of the transparencies that clump together after the
afternoon.
The way to salvation leads to a mine
and they are the muriskas who let themselves be led.

They have seen me in Cuzco, Cajamarca and
Arequipa.
The most daring ones dream of trapping me in their
lands.
I do not know if the larynx I studied yesterday
belonged
to a Bolivian or a Peruvian; I took it out intact from
the Titicaca.

They accused of stealing the tools of the miners.
And I boast of committing more sublime pranks.
Today I played in the navel of a pond
and in return I gave two gold nuggets as charity.
The blood of humanity is still dripping on the stones.
Then I stayed in the Uku Pacha.
The Twilight ends everything or begins everything.

YASY YATERÉ

(Lament of a Paraguayan teenager)

The whitish chest, iridescent hair.
A strange albino dwarf in the midst of solid brown
fosters
propitiate the excess of the innocent.

Lilith and Asmodeus were their ancestors.
The staff made of branches and gold obey them.
The glow is his friend when abandoning the moon.

You perceive the rustling of the leaf litter and it
observes you from the foliage.
It forces you to freak out while it plays its instrument.
It offer fruits and wild honey to your naked teens.

If you are a young man and you like it: kiss on the
mouth.
If you are a damsel: bite in the neck.
There are those who affirm that there is no light in
heaven,
that darkness is a ventriloquist and
Yasy Yateré is the best interpreter of his monologues.

There are also optimistic animals.
They think that the genie of the flute just intoxicates
with invention to control the masses
of anemic creatures that are lost in the heat wave.

Yasy Yateré attacks from the branches.
Yasy Yateré scares toads, parrots and tapirs.
Yasy Yateré does not take a nap.

THE ALLIGATOR MAN

(Existential Poem of a Colombian Alligator)

Some claim that I have the body of an alligator
and the head of a man.
I say that my thoughts are human:
vile network of black slogans.

Others say that I have the head of a man
and the body of an alligator.
I say that my heart is beastly:
anomalous vermin that swims in chaos.

One day I copulated with a nereid and her lips
were crystal flowers, leaving the swamp.
It was getting dark and we were still mating.
She groaned and I said "I love you".

I fell in love with the nereid and her light lips,
the subtlety of her settings immolating my scales.
It was the last night I saw her on the Magdalena River
and wandered on its banks to my own scorn.

Spectra fable their own legends
and project their frustrations into my life.
Intermittent snoopers that darken the day,
sad voyeurs feeding the night.

I think like a man and I feel like a beast.
When I become a man, I am depraved,
I produce the support of pale slogans.

When I become a beast, I am sensitive
and fall in love with the creatures of water.

When I become a man, I am the beast.
When I annihilate myself, I am the resurrection of the
swamps.
Am I an alligator with a man`s head
or am I a man with an alligator body?
When did I degenerate my nature and become a
human being?

Every day I fight not to turn into a monster.
I look for the nereid among the rubble
that originated the estuaries of pessimism.
From Plato to Bocas de Ceniza,
you will always see me on the shores of the Caribbean.

THE KHARISIRI

(Whistled ballad in the wind from Guaqui to Potosí)

Shadows fall and its entrails awaken.
(Lake Titicata is a hotbed of sounds)
The creatures emerge with a new skin.
(The wacanas, wac, wac, emit their squawks)

Chorus
Do not look at his eyes, his blond hair.
The demon of the plateau.
The demon of the Aymaras.
Do not invoke his name, do not say his name:
Liqichiri, Phistaco, Ñaqaq, Khari Khari.
The demons do not sleep.

Never travel alone on the trails of Achacachi.
(Sometimes he does not look fat but the marrow)
If there are no humans, he feeds on alpacas.
(First he steals your tool, then he uses your little machine)

The chorus is repeated
Do not look at his eyes, his blond hair.
The demon of the plateau.
The demon of the Aymaras.
Do not invoke his name, do not say his name:
Liqichiri, Phistaco, Ñaqaq, Khari Khari.
The demons do not sleep.

THE WHISTLER

(Monologue of a Venezuelan plainsman)

High-pitched sound driven by air
invade the silence and break the darkness:
fright arises, the hairs stand on end.
The night glows with darkness.

Whistle that breaks the music theory,
a wanderer creeps away
between the sheets of mist
proclaims the arrival of death.

His whistle is born as the fruit of pain,
scream of assassin, groan of parricide.
Cursed by their ancestors
he carries the skeleton of his parent.

He wanders on the plains on rainy days,
he walks through the plain in times of drought;
while he rests, a bark frightens him:
his dog Tureco follows him until the end of the days.

The whistle penetrates the ears and instills cold,
persecutes pregnant women and drunken people.
It is long and ungainly like a sickle.
He walks with his head downcast.

He wears a hat that covers his shame.
He has a bag that curves his back.
He faces a penalty that consumes him.
He has a pain that condemns him.

If the whistle is heard nearby,
do not fear because the whistler is far away.
If the whistle is heard far away,
the whistler is upon you.

He persecutes drunken people and womanizers.
He sucks the navel of the drunken people
to drink their schnapps.
He destroys the womanizers.

He does not rest.
When he allows himself to rest
counting the skeleton of his creator,
Tureco's howl terrifies him.

He skins the innocent people
and collect the bones
along with the remains of his architect.
If you are a walker, have your own dog.

The whistle is premonition of death.
Take care of those who walk
by the plains of Guanarito
or through the plains of Cojedes and Barinas.

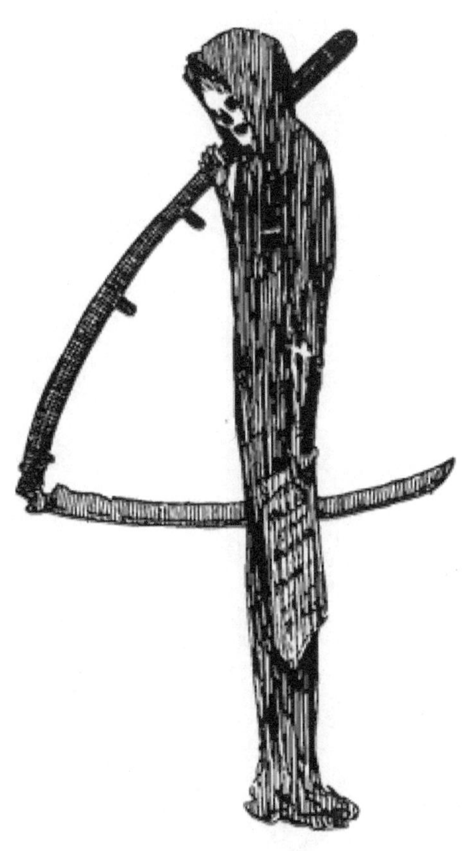

THE WIDOW

(Desperate song of a Chilean widow)

I got married with excessive love on a full moon.
My husband made me happy that night.

Confusion of love, moon and blood: they murdered
him.
I swore to finish off the line of homicides: I went mad.

I agreed with dark forces that promised to return him
if I complied with a series of nightly murders.

I did not hesitate and started planning the crimes,
looking for ethyl harlots, angry drunkards.

And I scream: You murdered him and I was so alone,
surprising their backs with my scary appearance.

I keep my feminine essence in my petticoats.
I am tall, I do not let people see my face through the
veil.

I stop steeds, carriages, cars,
motorcycles, boats from Chiloé to Puerto Montt.

I appear behind them, spectrum's kiss.
I strangle them in a hug of fury and passion.

I make the stallion slow down on the road.
The beast neighs and runs wild desperately.

I surprise the nape of the unsuspecting creature

and the horse is thrown towards the bottom of the
ravine.

I produce interest in the glassy eyes that look at me.
My hands and thighs are whiter than milk.

To the beautiful young men, apparently handsome,
I force them to follow me and their path narrows.

When packed lunches are scarce, I enter the towns.
Sometimes a post-mortem desire overwhelms me.

Burundanga sex, I numb them all.
I ride behind the riders I wish to be ridden.

To teach me the love arts
all the contortions tear me from death.

I tie the knights in the embrace of passion,
I take them to my hut so that they drink my water.

The ancients called me Lilith, and it doesn't make me
angry.
The ancients called me succubus, and it does not
overwhelm me.

Fateful lady, powerful ghost in a thousand ways
I have been called lost soul, widow, woman or witch.

Widow, spectrum, black angel, lonely woman.
Widow, ghost or horror. They have no way out.

The widow. The black widow. The widow dressed in
black.
Oh, what a pain: The love of my life died.

TELESITA

(Last vertical poem of an Argentine dancer)

Your last dance was the beginning of the dance.

Telesita, full of beauty and goodness
you took fire from the gods.

Your rhythm of folklore cremated the forests,
it ignited the passion in the cheeks of the ephebes.
The irony of fate married you to Eumelio Ahumado.
From your ashes the chacarera emerged.

Teresita del Barco, wandering and opulent soul:
the locals say you got burned at the campfire.
La Telesita, ghostly figure and beggar:
the matrons narrate the lightning bolt that broke your
dance.
Telésfora Castillo, lost soul and luminous:
everyone swears that you died dancing until you burn
down.

Telésfora Santillán, miraculous soul, complete
the ritual of the telesiada in Santiago del Estero.

THE CURUPIRA

(Anthropophagite poem of an amazonian hero)

I've been seen doing stunts on the lianas.
I dance every day between Pará chestnuts and acai berries.
Sometimes I ride a wild boar.

They have seen me cling to the trunks as an epiphyte.
My inverted footprints protect trees and beasts
and they distract the poacher and the barbarians.

Labyrinth of trees, the gardens of Curupira
where beasts are lost to find their place,
where lost places find nothing,
where the rain, the mud, the leaves,
mosquitoes and vermin live together.
Paradise of trees, the gardens of Curupira.
A paradise of songs and tones, effluvia and commotion.

I am the jungle that swallows the jungle.
I am the man who eats the man.
I am the beast that regurgitates the beast.
I am the word that undoes the word.
I am the black alligator and the glass frog,
the spider monkey and the bullet ant.
I am the toads that populate the swamps.
Come and meet me in the color of bromeliads.
Come and see how I swing between vines,
I slip through mosses and lichen,
I run away with my wild pig among the forest
and I caress the anaconda's skin
in the swamps of the Amazon.

CENTRAL AMERICA

TATA ELF

(Battle of dub poetry between Belizean elves)

Round One. Theme: Gods.
ARCANE ELF
My elf song is going to cause you troubles.
Your fragility shows my Titan´s size.
I am androgynous, a mixture of Faun and Aphrodite:
Penelope invites me to pose on her couch.

The jungle offers caresses of honeys.
Medusa is hypnotized and loves my voice.
I numb Bacchus, Horus and Cybele,
I uncover your pyramids and your Pandora's Box.

My hieroglyphs are rare and magnificent.
In the Pantheon you collide with my Olympus.
I walk alongside all the stars:
with Isis, with Aurora and with Freya.

KILLER ELF
I am a god, I am a true elf.
I don't need an Olympus, just green fields.
I am a demiurge of matter that transcends.
My feet upside down are the jungle where you get lost.

All deities of Teotihuacán and the Inca.
Itzamná and Pachamama form a mosaic.
I am the heights of Machu Picchu and Tahuantinsuyo.
I marry Inti with Ix Chel who makes her belong to him.

The chant to Viracocha also invokes Chaac.
I am the brother of Quetzalcóatl and Tezcatlipoca.
Buluc Chabtan is war; Tlazolteot, love.
Don't call me basilisk, call me your god.

Round Two. Theme: Duel of elves.
RESIDENT ELF
Do you need a cerberus piece of advice?
Listen to this old man
wrinkled and furry, with pointy heels,
resident in thunder, lightning and downpour.

My red hat shows off my beards:
my imposing footprint that the earth digs.
I am the brother of the toucan, the jaguar and the turkey.
Northern elves gave me the peyote.

The advice of this old man is not as wise as old:
Don't be perplexed: if you don't escape, I'll skin you.
You don't have my size, I invoke a Mayan shaman,
I eat magic berries and I win the battle.

CERBERUS ELF
I humbly accept your Resident admonition
so that you notice that my ego does not suffer.
If you want, I scare you with the mantle of my song
but don't ask me to tell you how horrible your crying is.

I also protect animals and the untouched jungle.
I search for the meaning of everything and nothing.
You: untamed as a storm; me: calm as leaf litter.
Southern elves gave me a dose of ayahuasca.

With my serenity I become a beast, never a human;
I become a boa and rattlesnake, in an American animal.
I am a brother of the tapir, the hummingbird and the
crocodile,
I am calm, not arrogant, I annihilate you without wishing.

THE CADEJO

(Costa Rican howl in times of hope)

Dark as Nix,
the Black Cadejo does not sleep.
The goat's feet pull the icy chains.

Eyes like bonfires, guardian of the trails,
the dog of the devil guards you
after parties, carnivals and disorders.

Explorers of canteens and games of chance
see their shaggy fur through the mist.
His eyes: it turns into tinder when they have contact
with the spark.

Antagonist to the shadows,
angel or guardian dog,
whitish like cotton,
albino like snow,
the White Cadejo watches you,
and watch your march
back to your inn.

They wander to the threshold of midnight
and are recognized in fierce combat.
Extreme collision at the margins of
the beginning of the day and the end of the night.

They are recognized in their mirages
made of dualities: right or wrong,

life or death, night or day, yin or yang.
Both return to the Poás volcano.

Noctambulant mothers
ensure that the Gray Cadejo
take care of sick children
and instills hope in them.

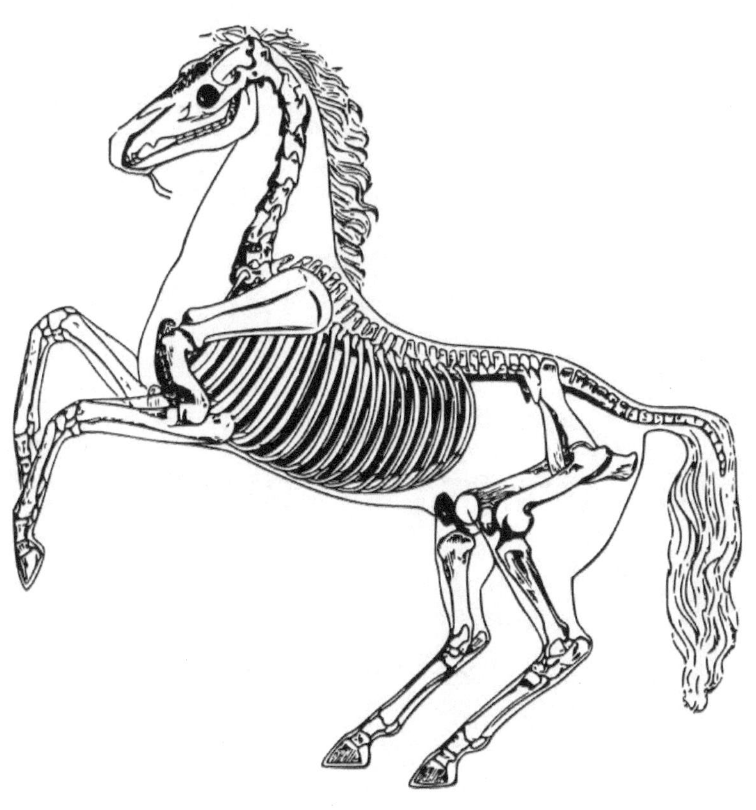

JUST JUDGE OF THE NIGHT

(Clandestine poems of a Salvadoran judge)

They say he hides behind the haze.
They comment that his head is smoke.
That when he punishes, he is dressed in black
That when he acquits, he is dressed in white.

They claim that he sparked the revolution of spirits,
the stir caused in the unions of hell,
that his dark revolutionary spirit told the truth,
that utopia is sometimes paid with the sentence.

They assure that he preferred the clandestinity of the
night.
For wanting to democratize life, they accused him of
treason.
Since those days of exile, he hides in the darkness
and whoever takes advantage of the shadows, lord
and master
it will be lashed without contemplation with the rod
of justice.

WITCH MONKEY

(Prayer for a Nicaraguan witch)

Gods
bring your glory to the woman who became a monkey
on all Nicaraguan nights,
who mutated in the shadows to satisfy her hunger and
the hunger of her people regardless of rumors.
You all-knowing gods know the tribulations she
suffered
like our unfulfilled dreams under the peaceful
moonlight.

That misunderstood woman shed her skin to find
sustenance.
She hung his hide on a tree and his body hair lushly
emerged.
Her hands and feet are lengthened and a big monkey
was laughing.

The short stature was no impediment to be
intimidated by his piercing red eyes.
The demons of the night paid her respect and
applauded when she danced.

She shed her flesh as she remembered the
recklessness she had to have when running around
in the roofs of the houses, and steal chickens to feed
their offspring.

Mona, those who loved her implored her, Mona...
don't furrow the night
transformed into a villain, with hairy skin to satisfy
anarchies.
Monkey...

Witch, those who hated her yelled at her. Witch...
stay away from our husbands,
we curse you a thousand times, they said between
anathemas and diatribes.
And the witch left the victims dumb for the rest of her
days
and the husbands only implored to meet Mona again,
with the Witch.

Witch monkey, you entered the forbidden corners of
reflections
and you forced to look at your face to those who did
not fulfill the duty of fantasy,
now you rest in the tranquility of nowhere.

When she came back swinging among the branches of
the trees and picked up his hide,
the Witch Monkey entered her slum and rested, her
long night began
and she will not change again, degenerate, mutate,
fulfill her metamorphosis.

Gods, lead Mona Witch to a new home,
to a Paradise where she never suffers human
transformation again.

NORTH AMERICA

THE HOLY DEATH

(Mexican words under the freedom of death)

I
I am Death, the sullen companion,
I illuminate the day of those who beg.
My actions are unique, they are not duplicated.
I am the Saint, and immaculate my scythe.

If you pray at night or at noon,
in the nesting maze or paradox:
I can do everything, even encourage life,
I can erase sadness and melancholy.

Give yourself to Holy Death and spend
your best hours on my glamorous cult
that I lead by breaking chains and hinges.

Show yourself attentive to my religious step
and when I pray I appear to you with my songs:
Day of the Dead and All Saints.

II
I was conceived by Ah Puch, god of the underworld.
In Xibalbá, a hidden place, they gave me the breath.
Fulfilling the pleas became a habit,
from birth I was ecstatic.

My tutors: Mr. and Mrs. Mictlan.
I learned to be neutral and dionysian at the same time,
they pray to me in Sonora, Yucatan and Oaxaca,
the ancients worshiped me in Tenochtitlan.

From the catacombs I emerged with a sure voice,
detonated the coalition of confused deities
dressed in the robe as the ideal armor

I dominated cultures, eras and ages.
Mature mythical goddess revered in every area,
in the steeds of the Apocalypse, an amazon.

III
My presence is considered demonic,
the pretense of mystifying scares them.
I am sincere, do not fear, my touch breaks
the evils of time, life hangovers.

Protective of the weak, I am matriarch of all,
in this chaos they cannot live without Death.
To pray they offer me flowers or brandy,
they light the candles and cheer to the Grim Reaper.

When they invite me, we drink tequila.
I am a sincere friend with my voiceless skull.
I am a skeleton and I mow the world with my sickle.

I can talk to everyone and my crow watches them.
The immense hourglass in my hand stands out.
I am the Most Holy and they also call me Skinny.

DEMON OF DOVER

(I sing to the demon himself)

1

I sing to you, oh devil, and I praise you,
and everyone should exalt the stealthiness of your walk
every atom of ours was formed in the cosmos,
stellar matter rooted to the ground.
You live ... and you circulate with your calm steps
on the grass and the stars.
You came from nothing and you will return to nothing
as creatures howl
and they don't understand the special stellar toughness
attached to the ether they sweat.
We are dust and we will return in dust
to the firmaments,
to the undiscovered spaces that will torment the wise,
to gurus and scientists engrossed in their doctrines and
lodges.
The night of the times falls and your silhouettes awaken
masked in the shadows
observed by the occasional witnesses
stepping on American soil
the exalted existence of your being
tailored to the nature of unprecedented cosmogony.

2

One night I saw you pass
you stepped slowly
with your long
misshapen arms,
and I have asked myself
since then

if my arms are not short,
the mutilated ones,
the abnormal ones.
You were walking impassively
with your glance
fixed on the calm
of Massachusetts´ soils.
The breeze hooted
over your head without proportion
and a smell of secrets came to me,
like little eyes
trying to understand
our filthy world.
A moment of discovery
that overflowed
all the facets
of the unexplored.
You,
me,
the orb,
all the existence.
Your legs were stretched and sometimes
they got together
with your hands.
You walked
almost hunched
due to the weight
of misunderstanding,
of the glances
snoops,
slanders,
opportunists,

those who don't understand you
and they think you're just
one more chapter of yellowing.
One night I saw you pass
and I met a pure being,
I met a partner.
3
I couldn't set
if it was the last century that welcomed you
with caresses of revelation.
Your genealogy is tracked
with the insistence of the shadows.
Mannegishi or Backoo,
I can invoke your names
who baptized the worlds for which
you slipped away insisting
in the presence of your long fingers
that adhere
to the names of creatures
of strange kinship
and the nomenclatures
of the modern demonologists:
Moth Man,
the Jersey Devil,
Loveland's Frogman.
They studied you in cryptozoology
and ufologists said that you were
a gray race alien
or a hybrid between animal and man.
But you are more terrestrial than trees,
more honest than birds,
purer than humans.

THE WENDIGO

(Short conversations about Canadian mythology)

They see it in the snow.
A spirit that mutates to the material in the icy wind
      /from the winter forests.
They comment that he possesses humans when they
are vile.
Some say he was a hunter who, when he went astray,
tried
      /human flesh.
His punishment was to become a monster of large
digits.
He leaves his mark stamped on the frost of the
      /trails.

Mossy creature that dwells in the recesses of the
      /forests.
Half fright, half human, thick fur, powerful
      /hands.
Sometimes it is the wind that hits the treetops.

The most beautiful legend tells the story of the first
      /Wendigo.
Betrayed by his beloved, he murders his love and
consumes
      /her heart.
The vital organ freezes and he begins to practice
      /cannibalism.

Gluttonous and anthropophagite, expert on voracity, excess and
        /craving are his company.
He never leaves a trace of the attacks and his footprints are never
        /heard.
If the Wendigo lacerates you, you will become obsessed with the consumption
        /of human flesh.

If you exceed you turn into Wendigo
If you practice cannibalism you become Wendigo.
If he owns you in your dreams you transform into Wendigo.

When he eats the meat of his victims, the proportion of his body
        /grows.
Famine, starvation, winter and cold are his
        /slogans.
Horrifying giant, they know him as Yeti, Bigfoot,
        /Mohan.

In the Algonquin tribes he is respected and feared:
The odawa, ojibwe, cree, kikapú, black feet, innu
        /abide by their walk.
He will live forever from the Rocky Mountains to the
        /Hudson Bay.

AMERICAS

THE GIRL WITH THE SCARF

(Anonymous voices of a Latin American suicide)

Located on a dark highway, the universe finds me to
make new stories.

*

Whoever has seen my shadow knows my most
intimate forms.

*

The nights commit suicide when boarding a car, the
cars pick me up as if I were an incarnate suicide.

*

Men fall in love with the unknown and when they
know it they tremble.

*

Voices travel the roads and seduce the lonely.

*

One night I got on a car, and it was red and the man
loved me. Men love what they do not know, and when
they know it they die.

*

The mist sweats secrets, the cold forces me to wear its
scarves.

*

Young people are attracted and in the morning my
shadow has left with the light of dawn.

*

Those nights we kissed in the cemeteries and the only
thing I took was her scarves and her calm.

*

Never look for secrets that you cannot bear.

*

On the day of the revelation they discover that I died
years ago and they tremble.

*

Hemlock is just the beginning of the journey.

*

I have also committed suicide from the tallest
buildings, they say they were the most beautiful
suicides in the world.

THE CRYING GIRL

(She chose the creatures of the night)

These were the creatures of the night:

They were called spectra, lost souls.
The creatures of the night.

Ghostly beings, afterlife gods.
The creatures of the night.

Apparitions, wandering visions.
The creatures of the night.

Evil spirits, frights.
The creatures of the night.

They could be invoked and they came.
They were called the creatures of the night.

*

Actions of the creatures of the night among men:

They were goddesses and demons
who proclaimed their presence with groans.
Under their skirts hunger and death were hidden,
sin, lust, the cries of the underworld.

Their skinned skulls were pierced by worms.
The eyeholes gleamed with vermilion madness.
They were of black hair and death-colored skin.
They were accused of infanticide and cried like mourners.

They traveled lagoons and plains, valleys and mountains
in search of bones.
It would end the regret by gathering the residue from its
offspring.
Oh, your children! Oh, your children!

Before going crazy they visited America.
They never remembered in which countries they were
born.
They never noticed under the light of which cities their children
were born.
They couldn't remember how many rivers drowned their
offspring.
Oh, your children! Oh, your children!

Since those afternoons they frequented the pools and
fountains,
rivers, lakes, and ponds, estuaries, and puddles.
They always wore their white outfits.
The one who saw their faces testified that they were horses
and that icy winds that froze his blood ran through him.
The wailing echoed for ever and ever:
Oh, your children! Oh, your children!

*

Nomenclature of the creatures of the night:

The crying girl could be invoked by sensitive people:
machi and calcu, some original shaman.
They called her in a thousand ways and it was all and one.
Auicanime, among the Purépechas,
Xonani Queculla, among the Zapotecs.
Cihuaóatl, among the Nahuas
(Mexica goddess who emerges from Lake Texcoco

to mourn for their children).
Xtabay, among the Lacandon Mayans.

In Mexico she was called Malinche and Chocacíhuatl,
and prowled the lakeshore
and the temples of the Anáhuac valley.

In Costa Rica they knew her as Itsö
and she projected pitiful screeches.

In Panama they nicknamed her Tulevieja
doomed to be a ghost
for murdering her unwanted child.

In Chile she was called Pucullén
and they accused her of throwing her children into a river.
They saw her many times in Rivera Park.

In Colombia they saw her with her hair adorned
with guinea pigs and butterflies lulling the corpse of a
baby.
They named her María Pardo or Tarumama.

Before the arrival of the white men
she was called Sakabiali, Mrs. Llorona del Monte
and Wíkela, child-eater.

In the plains of Venezuela they called her Sayona.
In Peru hundreds of times they saw her in the farms.
In El Salvador she wandered the rural streets wrapped in
moans.

Possibly she drowned his children in a river in Guatemala.
In Honduras she stayed for years and did not find them.
In Ecuador she found the little finger of one of them:

when she surprised infants she cut their fingers.

They heard her cry in Puerto Rico and Argentina.

She has also been called the Thirsty
She was older than evil.

She incarnated in Medea and Lamia as the Greeks attest.
She became a banshee as the Celtic testimonies affirm.
She was older than Rachel, Jacob's wife, according to
        /Christian mythology.

In Indonesia she was Pontianak, and she retained vampiric
features.
She was feared among the Yoruba towns.
In other latitudes they called her the White Woman or the
        /Woman in White.

Today the world of humans is no longer.
There are only the creatures of the night.
Philosophers destroyed myths and felt like demons.
Poets put an end to philosophy and felt like gods.
The gods combined philosophy and poetry and felt human.
Humans put an end to philosophy, poetry, and
        /myths and became nothing.
Only an echo resounds on the sidereal slopes:
Oh my children! Oh my children!

THE CHUPACABRAS

(American Anthem)

It happened some years ago, but I remember it as if it was
yesterday.
Hear the noise of broken chains and see the noble on a throne
        /equality.
I am the Chupacabra and I have claimed my place in America.

My vampiric virtues go back to the mammoths napes,
I drank his Pleistocene blood millions of years ago.
I crossed the Bering Strait with the first hominids.
The man appeared in the Holocene and I received him with my
        /fangs.
I hibernated for millennia and his lineage proliferated.

The drum and the siku were united to the strains of a new race.
I woke up next to the natives on the Caribbean shores.
I grew up in the dances of blacks, in the humidity of the
Amazonian
        /jungle,
in the desert plains of Atacama, in the icy blizzards of
        /Patagonia,
in the fierce gusts of Tierra de Fuego, in the arctic tundra of
        /Greenland,
in the jaws of volcanoes, on the majestic peaks of Los
        /Andes.

I was the scavenger of the aborigines attracted by their heinous
        /rituals.
The tombs are moved by the Inca and in their bones the fire
        /revives.
They saw me in Mexico and Quito throw me with tenacious fury.

And they cried bathed in blood Potosí, Cochabamba, and La Paz.

I condemned their heroes to cruel servitude and for a long time
        /they groaned.
Their names neither marble nor bronze at remote ages
        /will transmit.
This innocent and beautiful land was prepared for the fatal
destiny.
I am blood-sucking but I am not unaware of the charm of
        /anthropophagy.

The first children of the ground poured their blood for me.
I sank my fangs into his deep entrails
and they wanted to take revenge on the bloody monster
but my wings are more sublime than those of the condor.

I made empires succumb: to Incas, Mayans and Aztecs.
I dominated them riding my kisses in white armor.
I infected them with my regurgitated parasites on my verbiage.
The cross of my claws demonstrated the new doctrine.
I threw the yoke. The whole of America trembled with dread.

Dominated, the horrible night that spills the auroras ceased.
From its invincible light the American world is bathed in blood.
From the Orinoco the riverbed is filled with debris.
With blood and tears a river can be seen running there.

I am the legendary cryptid, the transmuted enigma,
the rumbling scream, a challenge to death itself.
I am the Chupacabras, giant by nature itself.
The Amazon circulates through my mysterious veins.
Between rivers and plains, between mountains and the sea
his bones in his land, heirs to his pain.
Wherever the ancestors are from
all life drags towards death.

I was also satiated in foreign fluids.
I raised the bloody standard.
The Chupacabras! They screamed. The Chupacabraa!
They come to his arms to slaughter their children and
          /companions.
All those beasts that ruthlessly tear the hearts of the
          /mothers.
To the people of America, infamous, three centuries a claw
          /oppressed,
and its echoes repeat the mountains like giants standing up.

They trembled in their arrogance in valleys, mountains and
forests
rumbling with fierce boom the caverns and the sky at the same
time.
To the roar that resonates around Atahualpa the tomb was
          /opened,
and savagely beating his skeleton in my palms, the blood that
          /waters the altar.

The blood of our parents, which sanctifies the soil, persists
in the proud Rio Hondo to the old Sarstún,
through the coral islands, over the Blue Lagoon.
I subdued the children of the Bahian clan by the Caribbean sea
under the limpid blue of the sky in the stubborn fight
that reddened men's faces.

From a country where the sun rises, beyond the bluish atlas
the fight was readied with wrath lying in the magnificent Andes.
Under my scarlet wing I lulled the beautiful quetzal,
my intentions are purer than those of the golden eagle and the
condor,
wrapped in his blood, behind the high mountain wild
          /hair

my great fangs shine like a bird with black plumage.

I wrote the legends with his blood.
Her story is painful and bloody.
Monstrous brothers, let us rebel
in this America in which indomitable dogs howl.
For our ancestors of the earth we are sole owners.
Let's walk together. Dying is beautiful.
Do not fear a glorious death.

Make your countryside with blood be watered, stamp your foot
          /on it.
And your temples, palaces and towers collapse with a horrid
          /roar.
The voice of the cannon will no longer roar or be stained with
the blood of
          /brothers.
We will have won the war. Our booty will be the sheep of
          /Puerto Rico.

The grave will belong to the free and your field is the happy copy
of Eden.
Majestic is the white mountain they gave you for bulwarking the
          /Heavens,
and that calm sea that bathes you promises you future splendor.
You see both seas roaring at your feet that lead your noble
          /mission.
They shouted: Deliver us from all evil,
be our light for countless hours.

Our slave chains were broken.
You can see, in the first light of dawn,
what we so proudly greet in the last flash of
          /twilight.
What is it that the breeze, on higher peaks,

whimsically undulates, showing and hiding itself at a
          /time?
Is it the terror of flight, or the gloom of the grave?
It's the Chupacabras!

Land of our ancestors, your temples are girded with glorious
          /garlands.
Our story is an epic of the most brilliant feats.
Creatures of the night and the sun.
Covered Lady, Muqui, Yasy Yateré, Alligator Man,
Kharisiri, Whistler, Widow, Telesita, Curupira, Tata Elf,
Cadejo, Just Judge of the Night, Witch Monkey, Holy Death,
Demon of Dover, Wendigo, the Girl with the Scarf, the Crying
Girl.
Creatures of the underworld, let's unite in this new era
in which humanity has degenerated and is the scum of the
universe.
America reborn. An sky which is always clear serves as a canopy
and it gives placid lullabies in the waves and swells.
Continental spectra, greet the new order
commanded by this American bestiary.

INDEX

CENTRAL AMERICA

TATA ELF
(Battle of dub poetry between Belizean elves)

THE CADEJO
(Costa Rican howl in times of hope)

JUDGE JUSTICE OF THE NIGHT
(Clandestine poems of a Salvadoran judge)

WITCH MONKEY
(Prayer for a Nicaraguan witch)

NORTH AMERICA

THE HOLY DEATH
(Mexican words under the freedom of death)

DEMON OF DOVER
(I sing to the devil himself)

THE WENDIGO
(Short conversations about Canadian mythology)

AMERICAS

THE GIRL WITH THE SCARF
(Anonymous voices of a Latin American suicide)

THE CRYING GIRL
(She chose the creatures of the night)

THE CHUPACABRAS
(American anthem)

www.traduzionelibri.it

www.diegomaenza.com